Collins

Treasure House

Pupil Book 6

Composition

Skills

Author: Chris Whitney

HarperCollins PUBLISHERS

Since 1817

William Collins' dream of knowledge for all began with the publication of his first book in 1819.

A self-educated mill worker, he not only enriched millions of lives, but also founded a flourishing publishing house. Today, staying true to this spirit, Collins books are packed with inspiration, innovation and practical expertise. They place you at the centre of a world of possibility and give you exactly what you need to explore it.

Collins. Freedom to teach.

Published by Collins
An imprint of HarperCollins*Publishers*
The News Building
1 London Bridge Street
London
SE1 9GF

Browse the complete Collins catalogue at
www.collins.co.uk

© HarperCollins*Publishers* Limited 2017

10 9 8 7 6 5 4 3 2

ISBN 978-0-00-823651-9

All rights reserved. No part of this publication may be reproduced, stored in a retrieval system, or transmitted in any form or by any means, electronic, mechanical, photocopying, recording or otherwise, without the prior written permission of the Publisher or a licence permitting restricted copying in the United Kingdom issued by the Copyright Licensing Agency Ltd, 90 Tottenham Court Road, London W1T 4LP.

British Library Cataloguing in Publication Data

A Catalogue record for this publication is available from the British Library

MIX
Paper from
responsible sources
FSC
www.fsc.org **FSC™ C007454**

This book is produced from independently certified FSC paper to ensure responsible forest management.

For more information visit:
www.harpercollins.co.uk/green

Publishing Director: Lee Newman
Publishing Manager: Helen Doran
Senior Editor: Hannah Dove
Project Manager: Emily Hooton
Author: Chris Whitney
Development Editor: Robert Anderson
Copy editor: Catherine Dakin
Proofreader: Cicely Thomas
Cover design and artwork: Amparo Barrera and Ken Vail Graphic Design
Internal design concept: Amparo Barrera
Typesetter: Jouve India Private Ltd
Illustrations: Leesh Li (Beehive Illustration), Dante Ginevra, Aptara and QBS
Production Controller: Rachel Weaver

Printed and bound by CPI Group (UK) Ltd, Croydon CR0 4YY

Acknowledgements

The publishers wish to thank the following for permission to reproduce content. Every effort has been made to trace copyright holders and to obtain their permission for the use of copyright materials. The publishers will gladly receive any information enabling them to rectify any error or omission at the first opportunity.

Macmillan Publishers Ltd for the poem on pages 16–17 'The Wind and the Sun' by Julia Donaldson, from *Crazy Mayonnaisy Mum* written by Julia Donaldson, copyright © Macmillan Children's Books, 2005; Egmont UK Ltd and HarperCollins Publishers for an extract on page 35 from *Flat Stanley* by Jeff Brown, text copyright © 1964 The Trust u/w/o Richard Brown a/k/a Jeff Brown f/b/o Duncan Brown. Illustration copyright © 2006 Scott Nash. Published by Egmont UK Ltd and used with permission; and Julie Holder for the poem on page 39 'The Loner' by Julie Holder, published in *Poetry Book, 3rd edition,* edited by John Foster, Oxford University Press, 1982. Reproduced by kind permission of Julie Holder for Leela; HarperCollins Publishers Ltd for the extract on page 69–70 from *The Football Shirt* by Catherine MacPhail, copyright © 2012 Cathy MacPhail; the extract on pages 72–73 from *Swimming the Dream* by Ellie Simmonds, copyright © HarperCollins Publishers Ltd 2012; the extract on pages 75–76 from *The Tempest* as retold by John Dougherty, copyright © John Dougherty 2015. Reproduced by permission of HarperCollins Publishers Ltd.

The publishers would like to thank the following for permission to reproduce photographs:

p.21 Leemage/Getty Images, p.28 NASA, p.32 Tetiana Yurchenko/Shutterstock, p.34 (l) John Chillingworth/Picture Post/Getty Images, p.34 (r) GL Portrait/Alamy Stock Photo, p.47 (t) outdoorsman/Shutterstock, p.47 (b) Lenar Musin/Shutterstock, p.48 (t) Vincent Amouroux, Mona Lisa Production/Science Photo Library, p.48 (c) Juniors Bildarchiv GmbH/Alamy Stock Photo, p.48 (b) Vibe Images/Alamy Stock Photo, p.51 (t) Clive Brunskill/Getty Images, p.51 (b) Clive Brunskill/Getty Images, p.53 (t) Ezra Shaw/Getty, Images, p.53 (b) Ezra Shaw/Getty, Images, p.60 (t) Lee Frost/Getty Images, p.60 (b) Visions of our Land/Getty Images, p.63 (t) Peter, Adams/Getty Images, p.63 (b) Per-Andre Hoffman/Getty Images, p.72 Natalie Behring/Getty Images, p.73 © Paul Thomas/Action Images.

Contents

Story planning

When planning a story, you should decide on settings, characters and plot. You should also try to have a clear idea of why you are writing. It might be just to entertain, but there are other things stories can achieve as well. Here's a plan Charles Dickens could have made for his story 'Oliver Twist'.

Read the text below, then answer the questions that follow.

> Stories can have many settings.

Settings

- a workhouse
- an orphanage
- an undertaker's shop
- London – Fagin's house
- London – Mr Brownlow's house

Characters

- Oliver Twist: a young orphan – the hero of the story
- Mr Bumble (parish beadle): a cruel man, treats Oliver badly
- Mr Sowerberry (undertaker): also cruel to Oliver, who is apprenticed to him
- Jack Dawkins (Artful Dodger): befriends Oliver, takes him to Fagin
- Fagin: a criminal who trains orphaned boys to steal for him
- Mr Brownlow: a kindly gentleman (revealed to be Oliver's grandfather)
- Bill Sikes: a violent criminal associate of Fagin's
- Mrs Maylie: a kindly lady whose house Sikes burgles

Plot

- Oliver born in workhouse – mother dies – grows up in orphanage
- Apprenticed to cruel undertaker – runs away to London

The magazine in which 'Oliver Twist' was first published; the readers were mainly middle-class British people.

Writing was Dickens' job. The more stories he sold, the more money he got.

Dickens also cared about social welfare and hoped his writing would inspire change.

Once you know what the aim is, you must decide how to achieve it.

'Oliver Twist' was published in monthly instalments. This made sure people bought the next instalment.

He believed the laws at the time kept poor people poor.

'Oliver Twist' was published from 1837 to 1839.

Believable settings, characters and dialogue

- Meets Artful Dodger who takes him to Fagin – sent to learn to steal
- Oliver framed for theft in street, caught by police – Mr Brownlow saves him, takes him home
- Oliver abducted by Bill Sikes – forced to burgle house – shot in act but rescued by Mrs Maylie, taken to countryside
- Sikes, fleeing angry mob, has fatal accident, Fagin caught and hanged for crimes
- Oliver reunited with grandfather, Mr Brownlow

Audience

- Readers of 'Bentley's Miscellany'

Purpose

- To entertain and excite the readers (and thereby sell more papers)
- To show the readers the terrible state of the poor
- To inspire the readers to make changes to help the poor

Strategy (how to achieve my purpose)

To entertain and excite (and sell more papers) I will:

- Create characters the readers will love
- Write scenes of drama and action
- Include action, tragedy and humour
- Introduce plenty of mystery, intrigue and suspense
- End chapters on cliffhangers

To describe poverty and inspire change I will:

- Use wit and humour to expose injustice
- Create a poor main character that readers will feel sorry for and want to help
- Set my story here and now – it's about the problems we have today
- Use realism so the readers know, even though it's a story, these things can and do happen.

Get started

Discuss these questions and complete the tasks with a partner.

Can you think of any books that you've read where the chapters end right in the middle of an exciting part? Can you think of any television programmes that finish their episodes like this? Discuss these chapter and episode endings. What was happening? Why was it so exciting? What is this type of ending called? What effect does it have on the reader or viewer?

Try these

Answer these questions about the story plan for 'Oliver Twist'.

1. Name two adult characters in 'Oliver Twist' who are on the side of good.

2. Name four cruel characters in 'Oliver Twist'.

3. What are the different settings in 'Oliver Twist'?

4. What should you consider when writing a story?

5. Who were the intended readers of 'Oliver Twist'?

6. How has this story plan been organised?

7. What were the reasons Dickens wrote 'Oliver Twist'?

8. Why does Dickens often leave Oliver in difficult situations at the ends of chapters?

9. What bad thing happens to Oliver after these good things happened to him?

   • Oliver runs away to London and meets the Artful Dodger but ...

   • Oliver is saved from the police by Mr Brownlow but ...

Now try these

1. What issues or injustices would you like to expose? Could you write a story to inspire your readers to solve or change things? Plan an inspiring story about something happening in the world today that you would like to see solved or changed. Copy and complete the story-planning table to help you. You can choose one of these topics, or use an idea of your own.

   • Saving the rainforest

   • Global warming

   • Child labour

Topic: (What will you tell your readers about?)
Settings: (Where is the problem you are writing about?)
Characters: (Include some nice and some nasty characters. Who is the main character? Who will the readers identify with? Will there be any misunderstood characters?)
Plot: (How will the storyline persuade or inspire your readers?)
Strategy: (How will you make your readers care about your topic?)

2. Authors often spend a long time researching the topic they are writing about to help them get the details of the story right and to help them decide exactly what it is they want to say. Spend time researching your topic and find out as much as you can about it. Go back to your story plan and check that all your ideas still work with what you know now. Make any changes you need to and add any ideas you have had as a result of your research. When you are ready, write a scene from your story. It can be the beginning, or any other scene that is particularly clear in your mind.

Summaries

A summary is a shortened version of a piece of writing which includes the most important details. Here's an extract from **'Peter Pan'** by **J.M. Barrie**. (Nana is a dog employed as the children's nanny.) Read the extract, and the summary of the extract, then answer the questions that follow.

On the night we speak of, all the children were once more in bed. It happened to be Nana's evening off, and Mrs Darling had bathed them and sung to them until one by one they had let go of her hand and slid away into the land of sleep.

All were looking so safe and cosy that she sat down tranquilly by the fire to sew. The fire was warm, however, and the nursery dimly lit by three night-lights, and presently the sewing lay on Mrs Darling's lap. Then her head nodded. She was asleep.

While she slept she had a dream. She dreamt that the Neverland had come too near, and that a strange boy had broken through from it.

The dream by itself would have been a trifle, but while she was dreaming the window from the nursery blew open, and a boy did drop on the floor. He was accompanied by a strange light, no bigger than your fist, which darted about the room like a living thing; and I think it must have been this light that must have wakened Mrs Darling.

She started up with a cry, and saw the boy, and somehow she knew at once that he was Peter Pan.

Mrs Darling screamed, and, as if in answer to a bell, the door opened, and Nana entered, returning from her evening out. She growled and sprang at the boy, who leapt lightly through the window. Again, Mrs Darling screamed, this time in distress for him for she thought he was killed, and she ran down into the street to look for his little body, but it was not there; and she looked up, and in the black night she could see nothing but what she thought was a shooting star.

She returned to the nursery, and found Nana with something in her mouth, which proved to be the boy's shadow. As he had leapt at the window Nana had closed it quickly, too late to catch him but his shadow had not had time to get out; slam went the window and snapped it off.

She decided to roll it up and put it away carefully in a drawer, until a fitting opportunity came for telling her husband.

Summary

Don't include unnecessary descriptive details.

If you use exact text from the story, put it in quotation marks.

English is simplest in the present tense so it's useful for writing summaries.

Never copy out whole sentences.

Paraphrase (use your own words) for the most efficient language.

The story of 'Peter Pan' opens when the children are asleep. Nana is out, and Mrs Darling has fallen asleep over her sewing. While she is dreaming about a "strange boy" from "Neverland", he arrives in the nursery accompanied by a bright light. Mrs Darling wakes up and immediately knows it is Peter Pan. She screams just as Nana enters . Nana springs at the boy who leaps through the window. Mrs Darling goes outside to see if he is hurt but finds nothing. On returning to the nursery, she finds Nana has trapped Peter's shadow, so she puts it in a drawer.

Dialogue can be written as reported speech to save space.

Get started

Discuss these questions and complete the tasks with a partner.

1. Think of a film you have seen and describe it to your partner. Listen to your partner's description of a different film. Discuss your descriptions. What details were included? What details were left out? What details were included that you could have left out? What were the most important details?

2. What is a summary? What should you try to achieve when writing a summary?

3. Write a summary of the film you described earlier. Pay close attention to what you include and what you leave out.

Try these

Answer these questions about writing summaries.

1. What are the five main points to remember when writing a summary? Make a list.

2. Rewrite these sentences in as few words as possible.

   a) All were looking so safe and cosy that she sat down tranquilly by the fire to sew.

   b) Mrs Darling screamed, and, as if in answer to a bell, the door opened, and Nana entered, returning from her evening out.

   c) As he had leapt at the window Nana had closed it quickly, too late to catch him but his shadow had not had time to get out; slam went the window and snapped it off.

3. What is direct speech? What is reported speech? Which is generally more useful in a summary?

4. Write a sentence to summarise each paragraph of the original text.

5. Summarise the summary by writing it as a list of events. Can you cut it down even more?

Now try these

1. Read this next extract from 'Peter Pan'. Then write a summary of it in no more than 50 words.

For a moment after Mr and Mrs Darling left the house the night-lights by the beds of the three children continued to burn clearly ... There was another light in the room now, a thousand times brighter than the night-lights, and in the time it has taken to say this, it has been in all the drawers in the nursery, looking for Peter's shadow, rummaging the wardrobe and turned every pocket inside out. It was not really a light; it made this light by flashing about so quickly; but when it came to rest for a second you saw it was a fairy, no bigger than your hand, but still growing. It was a girl called Tinker Bell.

A moment after the fairy's entrance the window was blown open by the breathing of the little stars and Peter flew in. "Tinker Bell," he called softly, after making sure that the children were asleep, "Tink, where are you?"

She was in a jug for the moment and liking it extremely; she had never been in a jug before.

"Oh, do come out of that jug, and tell me, do you know where they put my shadow?"

2. A blurb is a short description of a book, written to help people decide whether or not they want to read the book the blurb is about. Most blurbs summarise key information about the book, such as settings, characters, themes and a little bit of the plot. But the main aim of a blurb is always to persuade the reader that they really do want to read the book, so it can't give too much away. Choose a book that you have enjoyed and write a blurb for it. Summarise the key information and try to make the book sound really appealing. What information can you summarise about the book without giving too much away?

Adapting stories for plays

Well-known stories are often turned into playscripts for the stage or television. This extract is taken from **'Jane Eyre'** by **Charlotte Brontë**, published in 1847. Jane is an orphan. Her Aunt Reed, who has been looking after her, has invited Mr Brocklehurst of Lowood School to interview Jane to see if she is suitable for the school.

Read the extract from **'Jane Eyre'** by **Charlotte Brontë,** and the playscript adapted from it, then answer the questions that follow.

Uses dialogue and description to tell the story

First person; the narrator is a character

Mrs Reed occupied her usual seat by the fireside; she made a signal for me to approach; I did so, and she introduced me to the stony stranger with the words –

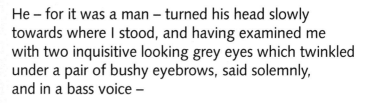
"This is the girl respecting whom I applied to you."

He – for it was a man – turned his head slowly towards where I stood, and having examined me with two inquisitive looking grey eyes which twinkled under a pair of bushy eyebrows, said solemnly, and in a bass voice –

"Her size is small; what is her age?"

"Ten years."

"So much?" was the doubtful answer ...

"Your name, little girl?"

"Jane Eyre, sir" ...

"Well, Jane Eyre, are you a good child?" ...

Mrs Reed answered for me by an expressive shake of the head, adding soon,

"Perhaps the less said on that subject the better, Mr Brocklehurst."

"Sorry to hear it! She and I must have some talk ... Come here."

Past tense; the narrator describes her childhood

Information in the novel that is absent from the playscript

I stepped across the rug; he placed me square and straight before him. What a face he had, now that it was almost level with mine! What a great nose! And what a mouth! And what large prominent teeth!

"No sight so sad as that of a naughty child," he began, "especially a naughty little girl. Do you know where the wicked go after death?"

"They go to hell," was my ready and orthodox answer.

"And what is hell? Can you tell me that?"

"A pit full of fire."

"And should you like to fall into that pit, and be burning there for ever?"

"No, sir."

This is how the extract from the book can be turned into a playscript. This is known as an adaptation; a text that has been changed to work in a new form or medium.

Scene: In the drawing room of Mrs Reed's house. She is seated by the fireside. Mr Brocklehurst is nearby. Jane has just entered and is by the door.

Stage directions are written in the present tense (because they are instructions).

Mrs Reed: (gesturing that Jane should approach) This is the girl respecting whom I applied to you.

Mr Brocklehurst: (turning his head to examine Jane) Her size is small; what is her age?

Mrs Reed: Ten years.

Takes description from the novel to use as stage directions

Mr Brocklehurst: (sounding doubtful) So much? Your name, little girl?

Jane: (sounding nervous) Jane Eyre, sir.

Mr Brocklehurst: (not unkindly) Well, Jane Eyre, are you a good girl?

Mrs Reed: (shaking her head) Perhaps the less said on that subject the better, Mr Brocklehurst.

Mr Brocklehurst: (more stern now) Sorry to hear it. She and I must have some talk. (He motions for Jane to come across to him.) Come here.

(Jane steps across the rug and Mr Brocklehurst places her directly in front of him. Jane is looking anxious.)

Dialogue taken directly from the novel	Mr Brocklehurst: No sight so sad as that of a naughty child, especially a naughty little girl. Do you know where the wicked go after death?
	Jane: (nodding yes) They go to hell.
	Mr Brocklehurst: And what is hell? Can you tell me that?
	Jane: (confidently) A pit full of fire.
Some stage directions have been added by the writer of the play.	Mr Brocklehurst: (sounding menacing) And should you like to fall into that pit, and be burning there for ever?
	Jane: (meekly) No, sir.

Get started

Discuss these questions and complete the tasks with a partner.

1. How easy is it to put these aspects of a novel into a playscript? Put them in order, with the easiest first.
   - What someone thinks
   - What someone does
   - What someone says

2. How have these parts of the novel been treated in the playscript?
   - "was the doubtful answer"
   - "was my ready and orthodox answer"

3. Which of these elements from the original text did not make it into the playscript in some form?
   - "usual seat"
   - "she made a signal for me to approach"
   - "Mrs Read answered for me by an expressive shake of the head"
   - "What a face he had, now that it was almost level with mine!"

4. What reasons might you have to leave out elements of the story you are adapting?

Try these

Complete these tasks.

1. Write these as lines of a playscript.
   - Fiona stared at him and said, 'Did you eat the biscuits?'
   - 'That is a problem,' Grandpa mused, scratching his chin. 'A dreadful problem.'
   - 'I won't say sorry, I won't!' screamed Penny, kicking the fence.

2. Match the feeling, as written in a novel, to the stage direction that could express it in a playscript.

   (Concentrating) (Trying not to laugh) (Shaking) (Sobbing)

   - She thought her heart would break.
   - I couldn't let him know that I thought it was funny.
   - John had never been so scared in his life.
   - Maria knew she had to get it right – it was so important.

3. Write a stage direction for each of these sentences.
   - Simret laughed as she read the note, threw it in the bin and set off for school.
   - Jake was bored. There was nothing on the television and he'd played all his games.

Now try these

1. Choose a book to adapt to a playscript and select a scene from the book. Make notes on any settings, characters and stage directions you will use.

2. Using your notes, write the playscript of your chosen scene. Remember to follow the rules for correctly writing and setting out a playscript:
   - Write the details of where the scene is set at the beginning.
   - Don't use speech marks to show who is speaking.
   - Write a name followed by a colon to show who speaks each line.
   - Start a new line each time a character starts to speak.
   - Write stage directions to tell the performers what to do.

Personification

Personification is a type of metaphor where non-human things are given human characteristics. Here are some examples of personification:

> the sun smiled
> the trees danced in the wind
> the flames climbed up the house

The sun didn't actually smile, or the trees dance, or the flames climb the house. Instead the writer is using figurative language to make these non-human things seem human. You can apply personification to an abstract idea such as hope or truth. Human qualities you can use include emotions, intentions and speech.

Read **'The Wind and the Sun' by Julia Donaldson**, then answer the questions that follow.

'The Wind and the Sun'

Said the wind to the sun, "I can carry off kites
And howl down the chimney on blustery nights.
I can sail boats and set windmills in motion,
Rattle the windows and ruffle the oceans."

And the old sun grinned
At the wild winter wind.

Said the sun to the wind, "I turn night into day,
Ice into water and grass into hay.
I can melt puddles and open up roses.
I can paint rainbows and freckles on noses."

And the old sun grinned
At the wild winter wind.

Said the wind to the sun, "You'll be sorry you spoke.
Down on the road is a man with a cloak.
If you're so clever then let's see you prove it.
We'll take it in turns to see who can remove it."

And the old sun grinned
At the wild winter wind.

The wind blew the trees till the boughs bent
and broke.
He bowled the man's hat off and howled round
his cloak.
He blew and he blustered, he tossed and he
tugged it.
The man wrapped it round him and tightly he
hugged it.

And the old sun grinned
At the wild winter wind.

"Take a rest," said the sun. "Let me shine on
him now."
He shone till the man started mopping his brow.
The man settled down in the shade of some
boulders.
He undid his cloak and it slipped from his shoulders.

And the old sun grinned
At the wild winter wind.

Julia Donaldson

You cannot apply
personification to a person;
they are already human.

Get started

Discuss these questions and complete the tasks with a partner.

1. Explain in your own words what is meant by 'personification'. Use a dictionary to check your definition.

2. Solve the riddle: I have hands on my face. I can't speak but I can tell you something. What am I?

3. Think of riddles for your partner to solve. Try to solve ones they think of for you. Take it in turns to solve each other's riddles.

Try these

Answer these questions and complete the tasks.

1. What two things are personified in the poem?

2. What human qualities can you use to create personification?

3. What human qualities are used to create personification in the poem?

4. Is it possible to use personification when describing humans?

5. How is the use of the word 'I' personification?

6. What abstract concept does each of these well-known characters personify? (Research them if you need to.) Copy and complete the table.

	The idea being personified	Description of the character
Father Time		
Mother Nature		
The Grim Reaper		
Lady Justice		
Uncle Sam		

Now try these

1. Explain why each phrase is an example of personification.

   • The stars danced playfully in the moonlit sky.

   • The words seemed to leap off of the page as she read the story.

   • The Christmas lights in the tree winked and sparkled.

2. Which verb provides the personification in each of the above examples?

3. Think of a verb for each of these inanimate objects to give them a human quality.

   • an avalanche

   • some car brakes

   • the moon

4. Write a sentence for each object or objects in question 3 showing the use of personification.

5. Write a descriptive paragraph, using as many examples of personification as you can, on one of these subjects:

   • a moonlit night

   • a storm at sea

   • a forest fire

Biography (I)

A biography is an account of someone's life. There are many types of biography of various lengths. Diaries, memoirs, and autobiographies are all types of biography. (An autobiography is a biography written by the person it's about.) Here's a biography of the famous novelist, Charles Dickens.

Read the biography and the CV, then answer the questions that follow.

Date and place of birth

Parentage

Charles John Huffam Dickens was born on 7 February 1812 in Portsmouth. His father was John Dickens, a clerk in the Navy Office. His mother was called Elizabeth. During his childhood he moved to London, then to Chatham and back to London again.

Places of education

Dickens went to Rome Lane School and then Clover Lane School until 1821. At school he was very fond of reading. His education was cut short because his father was imprisoned for debt. Two days after his twelfth birthday, Dickens found himself working at Warren's blacking factory. When his father was released from prison, he sent Charles to Wellington House Academy to finish his education. He remained there until 1827.

Profession

Place of habitation

Spouse's name and marriage date

Dickens then became a clerk for a firm of solicitors, learned shorthand and was promoted to court reporter. By 1832 he was writing for two journals and in 1833 he became a journalist for the newspaper the 'Morning Chronicle'. His job took him all over London and he enjoyed wandering about the city.

In 1836 he married Catherine Hogarth and in the same year he became a well-known author when he wrote 'The Pickwick Papers'. From 1840 to 1841 he wrote two more of his famous novels, 'The Old Curiosity Shop' and 'Barnaby Rudge'.

In 1842 Dickens went to America. He travelled to New York, Philadelphia, Baltimore and Washington, as well as making a short trip to Canada, where he gave lectures to wide acclaim.

Hobbies and interests

One of his main interests in life was the theatre and he organised productions of plays at Knebworth House and Rockingham Castle.

In 1857 he moved to Gad's Hill in Kent and toured Switzerland, Italy and France.

Major achievements

In the 1860s he wrote some of his best work, 'Great Expectations', 'Our Mutual Friend' and the unfinished 'They Mystery of Edwin Drood'.

Date of death

He died in June 1870 and was buried at Westminster Abbey.

A curriculum vitae (CV for short) is a form of biographical writing that gives a brief account of a person's life, concentrating on education, qualifications and occupations. A CV is usually prepared for job applications.
Charles Dickens's CV may have looked something like this.

Date of birth

Place of habitation

Places of education

Professions

Major achievements

Hobbies and interests

Surname: Dickens
Forenames: Charles John Huffam
Date of birth: 7.2.1812
Address: Gad's Hill, Kent
Education: 1881–1821 Rome Lane School
          1821–1824 Clover Lane School
          1825–1827 Wellington House Academy
Occupations: 1824 Warren's blacking factory
          1827 Clerk to a firm of solicitors
          Court reporter
          1832 Journalist – various journals
          1833 Journalist on the 'Morning Chronicle'
          1836 Novelist
Hobbies: Walking
        Reading
        The theatre
        Travelling

Get started

Discuss these questions and complete the tasks with a partner.

1. Explain in your own words what is meant by the term 'biography'.

2. Give three examples of types of biographies that you may have read or learned about.

3. If you have read any biographies, whose life were they written about? If you haven't read a biography, do you know of any?

4. What is an autobiography? If you don't know, use a dictionary to find out.

5. Discuss any autobiographies that you have read or learned about.

Try these

Answer the questions and complete the tasks.

1. Where and when was Charles Dickens born?

2. What was the name and profession of Charles Dickens's father?

3. Why did Dickens have to work in Warren's blacking factory?

4. Who did Dickens marry and when did he marry her?

5. What countries did Dickens visit during his lifetime?

6. Write a timeline of Dickens's life.

7. What details would you expect to find in a biography? Make a list.

8. What is a curriculum vitae? What does it concentrate on?

9. Why would a curriculum vitae not include details of the person's death?

Now try these

1. Plan your own autobiography. Copy the table and complete it with important information about your life.

Date and place of birth:
Where I have been educated:
Places where I have lived:
Achievements so far:
Major events so far:
Any other important information:

2. Now write your autobiography. Remember to keep chronological order, to write in the first person and the past tense, and to organise your autobiography into paragraphs. Include lots of facts about your life and you can include your thoughts and feelings about your life too.

Factual writing

Much of the writing we do is based on facts (information that is known or proved to be true) and there are many different ways of presenting a factual piece of work.

Read the two different accounts of a science experiment, then answer the questions that follow.

Kate wrote a report on a science experiment and typed it out.

A statement of the aim

Aim

To find out how much foam is produced by mixing detergent with different types of water.

Equipment

glass jar containing liquid detergent:
pipette
test tube
bung
3 glass beakers with:
river water
sea water
tap water

A set of instructions
(the order is very important)

Method

1 Half fill the test tube with river water.
2 Add 2 drops of detergent using the pipette.
3 Put the bung in the top of the test tube.
4 Shake for 10 seconds.
5 Leave to settle.
6 Record your results.
7 Repeat the method using sea water.
8 Repeat the method using tap water.

Results

Water type	Amount of foam in cm
river water	6.5
sea water	4.5
tap water	10.5

Conclusion

The tap water produced the most foam and the sea water the least foam.

Lynn has written about the same science experiment in a different way.

Narrative of events

We had science today and Mr Simms was not in a good mood. We had to find out how much foam you got when you mixed detergent with different sorts of water. Mr Simms had got some river water, some sea water and some tap water. He said he had been to the seaside at the weekend to get the sea water.

Reported speech

Paragraphs

We had to get out lots of equipment. We needed test tubes and glass beakers and this thing you use to drop the detergent into water but I can't remember its name. We also had to have a bung to stick in the top of the test tube. I like saying the word "bung". Our bung rolled on the floor and it took us ages to find it. Mr Simms told us to stop messing about and to get on with it.

Irrelevant to the experiment

Reported opinions

What we had to do was quite easy. The test tube had to have some water in it and then we put some detergent into the water using that thing. Then we had to shake it up. We forgot to put the bung in the first time so the water went all over and I got wet. Mr Simms wasn't very sympathetic! Anyway, the next time we remembered the bung and we made quite a bit of foam. I think that was when we used the river water but it might have been the tap water. I can't really remember. We had to do this with each type of water and I think the tap water made the most foam.

First person, past tense

Unreliable reporting

Get started

Discuss these questions and complete the tasks with a partner.

1. Explain in your own words the difference between a fact and an opinion.

2. Give an example of a fact. Give an example of an opinion.

3. How many suitable text types can you think of for reporting facts? Make a list.

4. Are some text types more fact-focused than others? Discuss.

5. Diary entries tend to focus on thoughts, feelings and opinions as well as recording events. Is the information in a diary entry always reliable? Are diaries unsuitable for recording facts?

Try these

The two accounts of the same experiment have been written very differently. Answer these questions about them.

1. What text features are present in Lynn's recount?

2. How has Lynn organised her writing?

3. What person and tense has Lynn written in?

4. What text features are present in Kate's science report?

5. What text feature does Kate use to emphasise the order of events?

6. Why does Kate use imperative verbs in the Method section of her report?

7. What imperative verbs does Kate use? Make a list.

8. How has Kate presented her results?

9. Which text is the most appropriate way to present scientific research?

10. Which text is most appropriate for a diary entry?

Now try these

1. Think of a science experiment you or your class has conducted.
   (If you can't think of any, think of one you would like to conduct.) Write
   a paragraph or two describing the experiment, similar to Lynn's recount.
   Describe what you did in the order that you did it, using the first person
   and past tense.

   Include answers to these questions about the experiment.

   a) What was the aim of the experiment?

   b) What equipment or resources were used?

   c) What did you do?

   d) What were the results?

   e) Did you prove or disprove anything?

2. Write a science report for your experiment. Set it out like Kate's science
   report: use the same sub-headings for each section; present the
   equipment in a bullet-point list; write the method as a numbered set of
   instructions; present the results in a table (if appropriate); write the aim
   and conclusion in full sentences.

Journalism

Journalism is writing and producing newspapers and magazines. People who write for newspapers and magazines are called **journalists**. Here is the front page of a newspaper.

Read the article, then answer the questions that follow.

LATEST NEWS

THE HERALD

ON THE MOON!

And It's "A Giant Leap for Mankind"

By John Barbour

21 July, 1969

SPACE CENTER – Houston – Two Americans landed and walked on the moon on Sunday, the first human beings on its alien soil.

They planted their nation's flag and talked to their President on Earth by radio-telephone.

MILLIONS ON THEIR HOME planet 240,000 miles away watched on television as they saluted the flag and scouted the lunar surface.

The first to step on the moon was Neil Armstrong, 38. He stepped onto the dusty surface at 9.56 p.m. His first words were, "That's one small step for a man, one giant leap for mankind".

Twenty minutes later, his companion, Edwin E. (Buzz) Aldrin Jr, 39, stepped to the surface. His words were, "Beautiful, beautiful. A magnificent desolation."

They had landed on the moon nearly seven hours before, at 3.18 p.m.

ARMSTRONG'S STEPS WERE cautious at first. He almost shuffled.

"The surface is fine and powdered, like powdered charcoal to the soles of the foot," he said. "I can see the footprints of my boots in the fine sandy particles."

Armstrong read from the plaque on the side of the Eagle, the spacecraft that had brought them to the surface. In a steady voice he said, "Here man first set foot on the moon, July 1969. We came in peace for all mankind."

AMERICANS FIRST TO WALK ON DEAD LUNAR SURFACE

ARMSTRONG APPEARED PHOSPHORESCENT in the blinding sunlight. He walked carefully at first in the gravity of the moon, only one-sixth as strong as on Earth. Then he tried wide gazelle-like leaps. In the lesser gravity of the moon, each of the men, 165 pounders on Earth, weighed something over 25 pounds on the moon. Armstrong began the rock picking on the lunar surface. Aldrin joined him using a small scoop to put lunar soil in a plastic bag.

Above them, invisible and nearly ignored, was Air Force Lt Col. Michael Collins, 38, keeping his lonely patrol around the moon till the moment his companions blast-off and return to him for the trip back home.

Get started

Discuss these questions and complete the tasks with a partner.

1. Explain in your own words what is meant by 'journalism'. Give examples to support your answer.

2. What do you think the job of a journalist might involve? Is journalism a job you would enjoy?

3. How important do you think journalism is? Explain your answer and give examples if you can.

4. Is it important for journalists to always tell the truth? Should they always present a balanced opinion?

5. Should journalists be allowed to publish anything they want to? Is there anything you think journalists shouldn't be allowed to publish? Who do you think has the right to decide?

Try these

When writing a news report, it is useful to plan by answering five questions. Answer these questions about the newspaper report on the moon landings.

1. **What** is being reported?

2. **Where** is this happening?

3. **When** did it happen?

4. **Why** did it happen?

5. **Who** was involved?

Newspaper reports also contain direct speech, or quotes, from the people in the story.

6. List all the examples of direct speech in the moon landing report.

Now try these

1. Imagine you are a journalist for a local newspaper. Plan an article for the paper based on one of these events:

   - A storm has hit a seaside town.

   - The famous pop group 'All Directions' performed in town last night.

   - The local football team 'The Reds' has won a place in the FA Cup.

   Invent a headline to catch the readers' attention. Plan your report by using the five Ws: What? Where? When? Why? Who? Decide who you will interview. These people will provide quotes.

2. Using the ideas and notes from your planning, write the full newspaper report. Describe the event as it happened and include quotes from the people who were there.

Review unit 1

Journalistic texts

A. Write a news report based on something that has recently happened in your town or village. Consider the 5Ws – Who? Where? What? When? Why? – as you plan. Use the planner to help you.

What are you reporting?
Where did it happen?
When did it happen?
Why did it happen?
Who was involved?
Think about your headline.
Direct speech I could use:

Writing stories

B. Choose one of the following titles and write a story with a clear beginning, middle and end. Write your narrative, considering carefully your use of paragraphs and how you link them.

- The longest day
- A strange tale
- At the water's edge

Use the planner to help you.

Title:	Who?	Where?	What happens?
Beginning			
Middle			
End			

Biography

C. Research information about an author whose books you like and then write their biography. Use the planner to help you.

CS Lewis

Malorie Blackman

Useful prompts:

Date and place of birth

Places where they lived

Achievements

Important events in their life

Any other relevant information

Now write your biography.

Humorous stories

A humorous story is a story that depicts funny characters or incidents. They're often about things that are impossible and because they are impossible they are funny, rather than disturbing. This is the beginning of a story called **'Flat Stanley'**.

Read the extract from **'Flat Stanley'** by **Jeff Brown**, then answer the questions that follow.

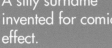

A silly surname invented for comic effect.

"I will go and wake the boys," Mrs Lambchop said to her husband, George Lambchop. Just then their younger son, Arthur, called from the bedroom he shared with his brother Stanley.

"Hey! Come and look! Hey!"

Mr and Mrs Lambchop were both very much in favour of politeness and careful speech. "Hay is for horses, Arthur, not people," Mr Lambchop said as they entered the bedroom. "Try to remember that."

"Excuse me," Arthur said. "But look!"

He pointed to Stanley's bed. Across it lay the enormous bulletin board that Mr Lambchop had given the boys a Christmas ago, so that they could pin up pictures and messages and maps. It had fallen during the night, on top of Stanley.

But Stanley was not hurt. In fact he would still have been sleeping if he had not been woken by his brother's shout.

"What's going on here?" he called out cheerfully from beneath the enormous board.

Mr and Mrs Lambchop hurried to lift it from the bed.

Reactions to Stanley's accident are all weirdly calm. This is a technique called 'understatement'.

"Heavens!" said Mrs Lambchop.

"Gosh!" said Arthur. "Stanley's flat!"

"As a pancake," said Mr Lambchop. "Darndest thing I've ever seen."

The story contrasts mundane family life with a bizarre event. The combination creates comedy.

"Let's all have breakfast," Mrs Lambchop said. "Then Stanley and I will go and see Doctor Dan and hear what he has to say."

The examination was almost over.

"How do you feel?" Doctor Dan asked. "Does it hurt very much?"

"I felt sort of tickly for a while after I got up," Stanley Lambchop said, "but I feel fine now."

"Well, that's mostly how it is with these cases," said Doctor Dan. "We'll just have to keep an eye on this young fellow," he said when he had finished the examination. "Sometimes we doctors, despite all our years of training and experience, can only marvel at how little we really know."

Mrs Lambchop said she thought that Stanley's clothes would have to be altered by the tailor now, so Doctor Dan told his nurse to take Stanley's measurements. Mrs Lambchop wrote them down.

Stanley was four feet tall, about a foot wide and half an inch thick.

When Stanley got used to being flat, he really enjoyed it.

He could go in and out of a room, even when the door was closed, just by lying down and sliding thorough the crack at the bottom.

Mr and Mrs Lambchop said it was silly, but they were quite proud of him.

Arthur got jealous and tried to slide under the door but he just banged his head.

Being flat could also be helpful, Stanley found.

He was taking a walk with Mrs Lambchop one afternoon when her favourite ring fell from her finger. The ring rolled across the pavement and down between the bars of a grating that covered a dark deep shaft. Mrs Lambchop began to cry.

"I have an idea," Stanley said. He took the laces out of his shoes and an extra pair out of his pocket and tied them all together to make one long lace. Then he tied the end of that to [...] his belt and gave the other end to his mother ...

Get started

Discuss these questions and complete the tasks with a partner.

1. What do you think makes a humorous or funny story?

2. Have you ever read any? What's the funniest thing you have ever heard, seen or read?

3. Discuss stories, cartoons, films and television programmes that you find funny.

4. Tell your partner a joke. Listen to their joke. Were your jokes funny? Why? / Why not?

Try these

Complete these tasks and answer the questions about the extract.

1. Describe in your own words what a humorous story is.

2. Give an example of understatement in this story.

3. Give an example of the use of contrast in this story.

4. If a boy were crushed in real life, how would you expect people to react?

5. How do the Lambchop family react to Stanley being flattened?

6. "Lambchop" is a silly surname. What do lamb chops make you think of?

7. What do you notice about the language the Lambchops use?

8. Which events in the story happen often in real life? Which events could never happen? Copy and complete the table with examples from the story.

Realistic everyday things	Things that could never happen

Now try these

1. Have you ever found yourself in a funny situation? Has a friend or member of your family ever told you about a funny situation or incident they were involved in? Why was it funny? Think about the situation and replay it in your mind so you are clear on the storyline. If nothing funny has ever happened to you or anyone you know, you will have to invent a humorous situation or think back to something you read or watched. Plan your story by thinking about the features of humorous stories you noted earlier.

   You should consider:

   • silly names or surnames

   • understatement

   • a contrast between the ordinary and the bizarre

   • impossible events

   • unusual behaviour.

2. Now write your humorous story. Use the notes you made previously and pay attention to the techniques you use to make it funny. Once you have finished, test your story on a partner. Give it to them to read or read it to them. Do they think it's funny? Were there any bits that didn't work? Make any improvements and then test it again on someone else.

Poems on similar themes

Poets may write about the same subject in a different way and you, as the reader, will respond differently to the same subject.

Read the two poems below, then answer the questions that follow.

The Loner

He leans against the playground wall,
Smacks his hands against the bricks
And other boredom-beating tricks,
Traces patterns with his feet,
Scuffs to make the tarmac squeak,
Back against the wall he stays –
And never plays.

The playground's quick with life.
The beat is strong.
Though sharp as a knife
Strife doesn't last long.
There is shouting, laughter, song,
And a place at the wall
For who won't belong.

We pass him running, skipping, walking,
In slow huddled groups, low-talking.
Each in our own familiar clique
We pass him by and never speak,
His loneliness is his shell and shield
And neither he or we will yield.

He wasn't there at the wall today,
Someone said he'd moved away
To another school and place
And on the wall where he used to lean
Someone had chalked
'watch this space'.

Julie Holder

The New Boy

The door swung inward. I stood and breathed
The new-school atmosphere;
The smell and polish of disinfectant,
And the flavour of my own fear.

I followed into the cloakroom; the walls
Rang to the shattering noise
Of boys who barged and boys who banged;
Boys and still more boys!

A boot flew by. It's angry owner
Pursued with force and yell;
Somewhere a man snapped orders; somewhere
There clanged a warning bell.

And there I hung with my new schoolmates;
They pushing and shoving me; I
Unknown, unwanted, pinned to the wall;
On the verge of ready-to-cry.

Then from the doorway, a boy called out;
"Hey, You over there! You're new!
Don't just stand there propping the wall up!
I'll look after you!"

I turned; timidly raised my eyes;
He stood and grinned meanwhile;
And my fear dies, and my lips answered
Smile for his smile.

He showed me the basins, the rows of pegs;
He hung my cap at the end;
He led me away to my new classroom ...
And now that boy's my friend.

John Walsh

Get started

Discuss these questions and complete the tasks with a partner.

1. What is the main theme of both these poems? Find examples to support your answer.

2. Do you have a favourite poem? How many more poems do you know? What are they about?

3. Copy and complete the table. Make a list of all the poems you can think of and what each poem is about.

Poem	What the poem is about

4. Do any of the poems you've listed cover the same topics, themes or issues? If so, do they deal with them in the same way or differently? Compare and contrast any poems that deal with the same topics, themes or issues.

Try these

Complete these tasks and answer the questions about the poems.

1. Copy and complete the table to compare the structures of the two poems.

	The Loner	The New Boy
Number of verses		
Number of lines per verse		
Rhyme scheme		

2. In 'The Loner,' what is meant by describing the boy's loneliness as his "shell" and his "shield"?

3. Make a list of the verbs in verses 2, 3 and 4 of 'The New Boy'.

4. What effect do these verbs have?

5. How does each poem describe the atmosphere at school? Are the descriptions similar?

6. Compare the endings of the poems. Are they happy, sad or something else?

7. How well do you feel you get to know the lonely boy in 'The Loner'?

8. Which poem do you like best? Why?

Now try these

1. Plan your own poem on the theme of loneliness.
   It does not have to be set in a school. Make notes
   on these things as you plan your poem.

   - Theme: loneliness

   - Setting:

   - Character(s):

   - Verses:

   - Rhyme scheme:

   - Powerful vocabulary:

   - Figurative language: (similes, metaphors,
     personification, alliteration)

   - Point of view:

2. Using your notes, write your poem on the theme of loneliness. When it
   is written, 'perform' your poem by recording it or reading it to a partner.
   Take feedback from your partner and do the same for them and
   their poem. If you have recorded your poem, listen back to it.
   What have you done well? Could you improve anything?

Extended stories

The longer a story is, the harder it is to keep track of its various elements. Long stories are usually broken up into chapters. Long stories need a good structure in each chapter as well as a good structure overall. This is why it is so important to plan a story. Here's a story plan for the first two chapters of a book called **'An Unusual Find'**.

Read these story plans for two chapters of a book, then answer the questions that follow.

Chapter 1

Setting	Characters	Plot
On a farm – kitchen scene where characters are having their breakfast: cheerful / bright / clean, old-fashioned dresser with dinner service, flowers on table	3 children: Sam aged 8 – rather timid, scares easily, not sure of himself. Small, red hair, freckles, dressed in shorts and football top Jo aged 10 – Sam's sister, tomboy, very confident, adventurous. Red hair very short, tall for age, dressed in jeans and T-shirt Martin aged 12 – serious-looking boy, elder brother of Jo and Sam. Wears spectacles, dark hair, dressed in jeans and checked shirt	Introduction – describe the scene and the children Conversation over breakfast – what are they going to do today? Reader must learn that they are on holiday at auntie's house. Bring out the children's different characters through what they say and how they act – Jo wants to climb trees. Sam and Martin are not keen.

Chapter 2

Setting	Characters	Plot
Same setting – kitchen	As Chapter 1 Introduce new character: Auntie Betty – middle-aged, cheerful, hard-working, always busy. Wears a dress and an apron. Hair long but tied up in a bun Anxious for the children to finish breakfast so she can clear away and get on with her work	Auntie Betty comes into the kitchen as the children are talking about what they're going to do. She suggests exploring and finding their way around the farm. Children agree
Move outside, describe farmyard		They go outside but can find nothing interesting until Jo spots the barn
Move to barn – cold and gloomy with rusting machinery, hay, somewhat run down		Jo eager to go in, Sam unwilling. Martin agrees but seems uninterested. Look around inside
Old cupboard, paint peeling off, looks discarded but is locked		Jo spots an old cupboard in the corner. Finds it locked and decides to break in. Martin warns her not to but she takes no notice Jo opens cupboard with a piece of metal – strange light and sounds come from opened cupboard

Get started

Discuss these questions and complete the tasks with a partner.

1. What books have you read with chapters? Think of examples of chapter books you have read.

2. Why do you think longer stories are divided into chapters?

3. Think of a book with chapters that you have read and describe the first two chapters to a partner. Listen to your partner do the same.

4. Discuss the chapters you each described. What do the first two chapters of both books have in common? What characters and plot elements are introduced?

Try these

Complete these tasks and answer the questions about the story plans.

1. What would you expect to find in the planning of the first two chapters of an extended story? Make a list by selecting the correct statements.

   • characters' personalities

   • direct speech

   • how the final chapter will end

   • descriptions of settings

   • character descriptions

   • structure of the whole story

   • details of the plot up to the end of the second chapter

2. Which three story elements have been included in the example plans?

3. What other elements might you want to include in a story plan?

4. Where is Chapter 1 set? Where does the setting move to in Chapter 2?

5. What character details are included in the Characters planning sections?

6. What must the reader learn in Chapter 1?

7. Who is the new character introduced in Chapter 2?

8. How has the author planned to end Chapter 2?

Now try these

1. Reread the story plans so far. At the end of Chapter 2, the author has planned for the children to find strange lights and sounds coming from an opened cupboard. What do the children find in the cupboard? Plan Chapter 3 under these headings:

   • What is in the cupboard: (make it something exciting)

   • What they do next/where they go: (invent a new setting)

   • Introduce a new character: (create a villain)

   • Chapter ending: (make it a cliffhanger)

   Write the chapter in full using your plan, to continue from the end of Chapter 2.

2. Plan and write Chapter 4, the final chapter. Plan the ending, deciding what type of narrative ending you want to use. Read it through, checking for effect. Is there anything you would like to improve?

Writing an explanation

Read the text extract from **'Extreme Animals'** by **Charlotte Guillain** and answer the questions that follow.

Life at the extreme

All animals live in habitats that give them food, water and shelter. Animals' bodies have adapted over thousands of years to help them live in their particular habitat.

Some animals live in the most extreme places on the planet. They have adapted in amazing ways to survive extreme heat and cold. Others live in very dry or poisonous places. They are nature's survivors, living life at the extreme.

Fact

Polar bears have thick layers of fat and fur to help keep them warm.

Feeling the heat

Deserts are the hottest places on Earth. Temperatures can become so high that most animals would die within minutes.

In the Sahara Desert, midday temperatures can reach over 50 °C. Most animals living there hide underground at the hottest time of day. But Saharan silver ants come out of their nests to look for food. They feed on the bodies of animals that have died in the heat. How do the ants survive?

Fact

Camels can live for weeks without drinking water.

The ants can keep track of the Sun's position to find their way back to their nests quickly.

Tough, silvery skin reflects the sunlight.

Special chemicals are produced in their bodies that help them to work in the extreme heat.

Long legs keep their bodies away from hot sand, and they can move very fast.

Fact

The lizards run on their back legs to get to top speed – four metres per second!

The hottest place on Earth

Death Valley in the United States is one of the hottest places on Earth. Few people can survive there. But fringe-toed lizards have adapted to live on the baking sand of the valley floor.

Scaly fringes on their back toes grip dry, loose sand when the lizards run across the hot desert.

The spade-shaped heads of fringe-toed lizards help them to burrow under sand and to cool down and hide from predators.

Flaps over the lizards' ears and in their nostrils protect them from sand.

The lizards don't drink water. They get all the water they need from food.

Deadly dry

Most animals need to drink water often. But some animals can live for a long time with very little water.

The central desert of Australia is extremely dry. Sometimes there is no rain for years. Australian spadefoot toads survive in this wilderness by burying themselves underground during times of drought, sometimes for years at a time.

Get started

Answer these questions in full sentences.

1. Explain to your partner, and then in a sentence, what it means to live life at the extreme.

2. Name the extreme kind of habitat mentioned in the extract.

3. Name two of the hottest places on the planet.

4. Give examples of animals mentioned as survivors.

5. Explain the meaning of the word 'adapt' in this extract.

Try these

1. Explain how speed has helped the fringe-toed lizard to adapt to life in the desert.

2. What technical language do you find in the information about the fringe-toed lizard?

3. What verb tense is used in the information about the lizard?

4. What organisational device helps to organise the information about the fringe-toed lizard?

5. What is the role of the titles in this explanation text?

Now try these

1. Research facts about adaptation to extreme cold and write a paragraph explaining how animals adapt to this type of habitat.

2. What other examples of extreme habitat can you think of? Research one of these habitats and create a fact file called 'Extreme Survivors'. Your fact file should include a heading, subheadings, at least one labelled diagram or illustration, and a box containing an exciting or 'fun' fact. Include information about animals who survive the new extreme you've researched, the extreme cold you wrote about in question 1 and the extreme heat you read about in the extract.

Paragraphs in non-fiction

Longer pieces of text should be divided into **paragraphs**. A paragraph is a section of text indicated by a new line. It usually comprises more than one sentence and deals with a single theme, topic or idea. Each paragraph usually has two or more sentences related to the same idea.

Read these information texts, then answer the questions that follow.

Usain Bolt

Paragraphs organise information and break up the text into readable chunks.

Jamaican sprinter Usain bolt is arguably the fastest man in the world, winning three gold medals at the 2008 Olympic Games in Beijing, China, and becoming the first man in Olympic history to win both the 100 m and 200 m races in record times. He continued his run of success by winning three gold medals at the London 2012 Olympics, defending both of his sprint titles – 100 and 200 metres – and, with his team mates, retaining the 4×100 m relay title in a world record time of 36.84 seconds.

Usain's early life

Bolt's successes are listed chronologically.

He was born in Jamaica on 21 August, 1986. From a young age, he was a very good cricketer as well as a remarkable young sprinter. By the age of 14, Bolt had won his first school championships medal, taking the silver in the 200 m race.

At the age of 15, Bolt won his first international competition at the 2002 World Junior Championships. He won the 200 m race, making him the youngest world-junior gold medal winner ever! People realised he was a very special athlete and he soon was given the nickname Lightning Bolt!

His running career

Despite being constantly troubled by injury, he was chosen for the Jamaican Olympic squad for the 2004 Olympics but was eliminated in the first round due to that recurring injury.

In 2005, he made the difficult decision to move to a new coach, Glenn Mills. This was a good move but, unfortunately, injuries continued to be a problem.

But by 2007 things were improving. First, he broke the 30-year-old Jamaican 200 m record and then won two silver medals at the World Championships in Japan.

Bolt strikes gold

At the Beijing Olympics in 2008, Usain broke the 100 m world record, winning in 9.69 seconds. Not only did he run a very fast time, but everyone was amazed that he slowed down to celebrate before he finished! He also won gold medals in the 200 m race and in the relay.

At the 2012 Olympic Games in London, he won his fourth Olympic gold medal in the men's 100 m race, beating his friend and rival Yohan Blake. This was not a new Olympic record. The win marked Bolt's second consecutive gold medal in the 100 m.

He went on to compete in the men's 200 m, claiming his second consecutive gold medal in that race too. He was awarded his third gold medal as part of the Jamaican relay team.

Bolt expressed his pride about his 2012 performance, saying, "It's what I came here to do. I've got nothing left to prove."

New section of text, indicated by the heading

Space between paragraphs

Mo Farah

Although Mohamed Farah was born in Mogadishu on 23 March 1983, his father had been born in England and had met his mother when on holiday in Somalia. Mo moved to London when he was eight years old. His first love was football, but it was his speed on the pitch that showed a special talent for running. (More than anything Mo dreamed of playing for Arsenal!) When he was 13, Mo came ninth in the English schools cross country competition, but by the following year he won – and went on to win four more English school titles. In 2005, Mo Farah made the important decision to move in with a group of Kenyan runners that included 10,000 m world number one Micah Kogo. "I don't just want to be British number one, I want to be up there with the best," said Mo. Soon after, he became Britain's second-fastest 5000 m runner and came second in the European Championships before winning the European Cross-Country Championship in Italy. The 2008 Olympics weren't good for Mo, but he really started to improve dramatically after going to Ethiopia and Kenya for training. He set a new British indoor record in the 3000 m. Soon after, he broke his own record by more than six seconds, which commentator Steve Cram called "the best performance by a male British distance runner for a generation". However, he became unwell after several races and it was eventually found that he had low levels of important chemicals in his blood. Once this was sorted out, he started to win more important races. He won the 2010 London 10,000 m in a British record and the following week he won the European Cup 10,000 m and then the 2010 European Athletics Championships, where he took the 10,000 m gold medal. 2011 proved to be a highly successful year.

In January he won the Edinburgh Cross Country. Then in February 2011, he moved to the USA, to work with his new coach. He went on to win major races all over the world. Dave Moorcroft, former 5000 m world-record holder, described Farah as "the greatest distance runner that Britain has ever seen". On 4 August 2012, he won the 10,000 m gold, Great Britain's first ever Olympic gold medal in the 10,000 m. A week later Farah made it a long-distance double, winning the 5000 m. This was when millions of people all over the world saw Mo's unique victory celebration dance – the Mobot!

Get started

Discuss these questions and complete the tasks with a partner.

1. Explain in your own words what is meant by the term 'paragraph'.

2. Why is it important to use paragraphs in non-fiction writing?

3. Look back at your previous writing and find examples of when you used paragraphs and explain why you used them.

4. Discuss whether your reasons are the same for fiction and non-fiction.

5. Make a checklist for the use of paragraphs in non-fiction. Use the annotations on the extracts for help if you need to.

Try these

Complete these tasks and answer the questions about the texts.

1. How many headings are there in the text about Usain Bolt?

2. How many paragraphs are there in the text about Usain Bolt?

3. Write a sentence to summarise each section of the text about Usain Bolt.

4. Look at the text on Mohamed Farah. What is wrong with it?

5. How would you break up the information in the text on Mohamed Farah? Copy the table and add these headings to it in the correct order. One has been done for you. Then specify where you think each paragraph break should go.

- British records and European champion
- 2012: Double Olympic champion
- His ambition grows
- Mo's early life
- Britain's greatest male distance runner

Heading	Information to be included in this section
Mo's early life	Up to "... English school titles"

Now try these

1. Plan an information text about your favourite hobby or sport. The facts for your information text need to be organised into sections. Here is a diagram with ideas for the different sections of your information text. Copy the diagram and fill in any or all of the sections with information about your chosen hobby or sport. Add other sections with ideas of your own if you want to. Research your hobby or sport if you need to and check that the information is accurate and correct.

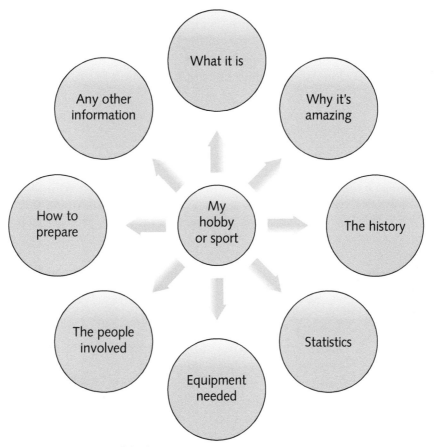

Once you have added all the information you want to include in your text, decide the order in which you want to write the information. Label each section with a number according to the order in which you're going to write the information.

2. Using your plan, write an information text about your chosen hobby or sport. Use the checklist you composed to make sure you are using sections and paragraphs correctly.

Paragraphs in fiction

Paragraphs are used in fiction writing whenever the narrative changes time, place, topic or speaker, or when the writer wants to control the pace of the narrative and create dramatic effects.

Read the story extract, then answer the questions that follow.

Our New Home

Mum closed the car door. Everything had been packed into the car, including us, and it was time to go. I felt a rush of emotions as the car pulled out of the drive. We were leaving our home. I was 15 years old and had lived in that house all of my life.

> **Change in topic (also change in time)**

When dad disappeared, mum said we couldn't afford to live there anymore. I had tried to argue with her, talk her out of moving away, but she told me there was no point. These were the facts, she'd said, and we all had to face them.

> **A very short paragraph for dramatic effect; it is a moment of heightened emotion**

I watched as the house seemed to disappear behind a mist of fog. In fact, it wasn't fog; they were my tears.

The day seemed to roll by as we travelled along the motorway. My younger brother Kirk, he was only five, kept on tapping his hand against the window. He was playing some sort of game and to be honest the sound was really annoying. Mum didn't say anything though. She hadn't spoken since we left the house.

She hadn't spoken much at all these last few months. It was like the breath had been knocked out of her. Looking at her sideways, from the passenger seat next to her, I tried to work out how much she'd really changed. Was she as different as I thought? Or did I just see her differently now?

Character begins to speak

"Mum ..." I began. But she just drove, quietly humming to herself. It wasn't a real tune; it was just a sound. More like a stifled groan. I put my headphones on and turned up my music.

Different time

It was getting dark. We would soon be there, at "our new home," as Mum kept on calling it. I didn't want a new home. I wanted the old one with all of my friends and with Mr Andrews's grumpy dog jumping over the back fence. In fact, Mr Andrews was grumpier than his dog. The only difference was that he hadn't learned to bark yet. I smiled to myself. It's funny the things you miss.

Different place

We pulled into the drive. At last Kirk was quiet. Perhaps he was secretly nervous too, behind all of that dribble and noise, about beginning a new life. I looked up at the new house through the car window. What would our new lives be like?

Get started

Discuss these questions and complete the tasks with a partner.

1. Look back at your previous writing and find examples of when you used paragraphs in fiction writing. Explain why you used them.

2. Make a checklist for the use of paragraphs in fiction writing. Read the notes and annotations of the extract for further support, if you need to.

3. Look at examples of fiction texts (in books you are reading or that are available to you). What is the shortest paragraph you can find? What is the longest paragraph you can find? What effect do short paragraphs have? What effect do long paragraphs have? Can you identify the reasons for paragraph breaks in the texts you are looking at? Are there any you don't understand? Are there any you disagree with?

Try these

1. Copy and complete the table. For each paragraph of the story, write the first sentence and the reason for starting a new paragraph.

	First sentence	Reason for starting a new paragraph
Paragraph 2		
Paragraph 3		
Paragraph 4		
Paragraph 5		
Paragraph 6		
Paragraph 7		
Paragraph 8		

2. What happens next? Write the next three paragraphs of the story. Use your checklist to help you remember when to start a new paragraph. Make a note of your reason for each paragraph break.

Now try these

1. In this narrative extract, the paragraph breaks have been omitted.
   Using the line numbers, suggest where you think the paragraph breaks
   should happen and give your reasons.

1	It was a cold, damp day. The rain had been falling all morning and
2	there had been no chance of going out at all. Kamal really wanted
3	to meet his friends and play football. But here he was, stuck inside
4	with no sign of brighter weather. He would have to stay indoors and
5	watch the television. All of a sudden the phone rang in the other
6	room and he ran to answer it. It was his cousin, Hamid, asking him to
7	come over to play on his new computer game. It had been a present
8	for his birthday and he was longing for someone to play it with him.
9	The offer was irresistible! Kamal agreed, promising to be there in
10	half an hour. He rushed to the hall to get his coat and search for his
11	trainers. It was then he remembered the hole! The last time he wore
12	his trainers playing football he had noticed large holes in the soles of
13	both trainers, made worse by continually playing football! His feet
14	would get soaked but that new game was something special and
15	he couldn't resist the invitation. He put them on, opened the door
16	and rushed outside. Rain fell in sheets, and a cold wind blew, but
17	still Kamal ran on to his cousin's house. By the time he reached the
18	end of his road, his feet were soaked through. His socks were wet,
19	his toes were freezing cold and he felt sure there was a blister on his
20	left heel. He saw his cousin's house in the distance and leaping over
21	puddles like small lakes he finally rang the door bell. "Hello Kamal,"
22	said his cousin. "You'd better come in and get dry. I don't know what
23	we can do though; there's been a power cut due to the storm and
24	the computer isn't working." The look on Kamal's face said it all.
25	Cold, wet and no computer game. What a day!

2. Write your own short story.
   Your paragraphs must structure the story.
   Use your checklist to help you. Choose
   one of these titles or use one of your own:

   • The lost purse

   • The match

   • Aliens in the High Street!

Writing for different purposes

When you have researched a topic, there are different ways to convey factual information including diaries, letters, reports, newspaper articles, maps and diagrams. The method chosen depends on who will be reading it and what they need to know. Here are three different ways of giving information about Morocco.

Read the information on Morocco, then answer the questions that follow.

From an information book

Use of semicolons

Full sentences

Sub-headings

Morocco

Location

The name Morocco comes from the old Arabic phrase "Maghreb al-Aksa" meaning "The Land of the Furthest West"; Morocco is, in fact, at the extreme western corner of North Africa. It is the only North African country with a coast facing the Atlantic Ocean, and of all the North African countries, it is the nearest to Europe. The country is bordered inland by Algeria, and for a much shorter distance by Western Sahara.

Size

The area of Morocco is 440,000 square kilometres (170,000 square miles). This is just a little more than twice as large as the area of the British Isles.

The mountains

Well over one-third of Morocco is mountainous. In the north are the Rif Mountains; further south are the Middle Atlas, the High Atlas and the Anti Atlas. All these ranges, except the Rif, run roughly southwest to northeast across the country. In the east, the Middle Atlas and High Atlas merge to form a barren tableland.

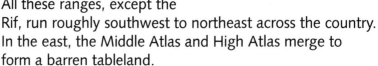

From an atlas

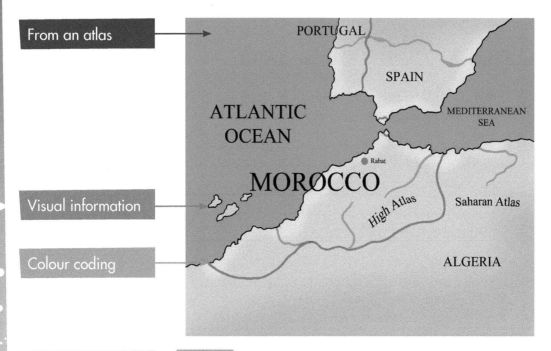

Visual information

Colour coding

From a reference book

Morocco

A list of statistics

Population: about 20 million

Main languages: Arabic and French

Main religion: Islam

Capital: Rabat

Area: 440,000 square kilometres (170,000 square miles)

Highest mountain: Tidiguin: 2,400 metres

Information is organised using a colon.

Chief produce: fruit (oranges and figs), cereals

Get started

Discuss these questions and complete the tasks with a partner.

1. Think of as many different ways to present information as you can. Make a list.

2. How do you know which method to use when presenting information? What are the advantages and disadvantages of the different ways you have thought of?

3. When and how can you use a colon? Write the rules. (If you're not sure about them, look them up.)

4. When and how can you use a semicolon? Write the rules. (If you're not sure about them, look them up.)

Try these

Answer these questions.

1. What are the advantages of using a map to present information?

2. What are the disadvantages of using a map to present information?

3. What do the pictures in the information book extract show the reader?

4. What facts are included in the information book extract? Make a list.

5. What three pieces of information can only be found in the map?

6. What piece of information is in both the information book extract and the reference book?

7. What could be added to the map to give the reader an idea of the size of Morocco?

8. Which extract uses colons to organise information?

9. What are the sub-headings for in the information book extract?

Now try these

1. Imagine you work for the Moroccan tourist board and you have to write an information leaflet promoting Morocco as a place to visit. Read through the information in the extracts provided and, if possible, do your own research and make notes about places to visit and things to do while in Morocco. Your leaflet should encourage visitors to come and see Morocco. What facts and information will you include to make people want to visit? Decide what the sections will be and how you will present the information leaflet. Consider layout, maps, illustrations, bullet point lists and anything else you can think of.

2. Write the leaflet, referring to the notes you made earlier. Remember, you want people to visit Morocco so use persuasive language and tell them enticing things. Use organisational features to format the information you're providing. Think carefully about how you present the different types of information. Try to make your leaflet as reader-friendly and usable as possible.

Poems on a theme

A. Write a poem on a theme of your choice. Use the planner to help you.

Theme: _____

Title: _____

Checklist:

Setting

Character(s)

Verses

Rhyme or not

Powerful vocabulary

Simile/metaphor or personification

first or third person?

Write your poem

Paragraphs in non-fiction

B. Choose one of the following titles and make notes on the content of each paragraph in your non-fiction report.

- Space

- Dance

- Horses

Use the planner to help you.

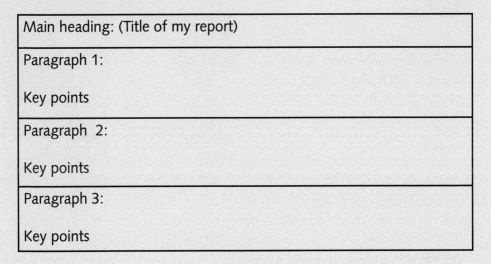

Main heading: (Title of my report)
Paragraph 1: Key points
Paragraph 2: Key points
Paragraph 3: Key points

Story endings

C. Write an alternative ending to a traditional tale.

1. What has happened in the story so far?
2. Write the alternative ending.

Story endings

How you, as a reader, feel when you finish a story depends on how the story ends. Writers know how they want to make their readers feel and they write the endings to their stories to produce these feelings. Here is a plan for a story called **'The Mountain Climbers'**.

Read the story plan, then answer the questions that follow.

Beginning

Three climbers are half way up a mountain when one falls. He is saved from plummeting to the bottom by a ledge, but his leg is broken.

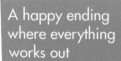

Middle

The three climbers spend an uncomfortable night on the mountain. The temperature drops and the man with the broken leg becomes very ill. Rescue is a remote possibility because, foolishly, they didn't tell anyone they were going climbing.

A happy ending where everything works out

Ending

Do you want to leave your reader with a sense of relief?

One climber has a flare so the climbers are rescued.

A cliffhanger ending (a dramatic ending to a story that maintains suspense)

Do you want to leave your reader in suspense?

Two of the climbers go down the mountain to get help, leaving the injured man alone. Will they return?

Do you want to leave your reader with a sense of "if only"?

A sad ending

A rescue party does arrive but too late to save the injured man.

Get started

Discuss these questions and complete the tasks with a partner.

1. Describe some endings of stories you have read, watched or listened to.

2. Which endings did you like best? Do you prefer happy endings or sad endings? Do you enjoy a good cliffhanger? Have you enjoyed any mysterious endings that have left you with questions unanswered?

3. Write a few sentences explaining how you like stories to end. Is a happy ending always the best ending?

Try these

What do you know about story endings?

1. Write a definition of the term 'cliffhanger'.

2. What is a 'prequel'? What is a 'sequel'?

3. Some stories are called 'cyclical'. What do you think this means for the ending of the story?

4. What is an 'ambiguous' ending?

5. What sorts of endings are most suitable for young children?

6. Copy and complete the table, describing how you might expect a story in each of these genres to end.

	How the story might end
A fairytale	
A murder mystery	
A romance	
A moral story	
A tragedy	
A comedy	
A survival story	

Now try these

1. Reread the three possible endings to 'The Mountain Climbers'. Think of another way the story could end. What effect will it have on the reader? Write a short description of what happens.

Choose what you think is the best ending, one of the three suggestions or your own, and complete the story 'The Mountain Climbers' in full. Read it through, making sure that it creates the effect you wanted. Share the ending with a partner and listen to their feedback. Do the same for your partner's story ending.

2. Think of a story you have read, watched or listened to where you really didn't like the ending. Write a review of the story, explaining exactly why you didn't like the ending. Here are some questions to help you decide why you didn't like it:

   • Did the ending make sense?

   • Do you think it was planned well enough?

   • Did it seem false or not to fit with the rest of the story somehow?

   • Was it too sudden or abrupt, or just not really an ending at all?

   • Was it too complicated? Did too much happen at once?

   • Was the problem that questions were left unanswered and loose ends not tied up? If so, do you think that was deliberate or a mistake made by the author?

   • Is it just a matter of personal taste?

Narrative writing

Read the extract from **'The Football Shirt'** by **Catherine MacPhail and Paul Fisher**, and then answer the following questions.

LOCAL BOY DIES IN CRASH

Local boy, Thomas Tully, was killed today when his motorbike hit a tree on the main road going out of town

Ross first saw the football shirt that Wednesday morning. It was pinned on the tree by the roadside. There was a football scarf wound round one of the branches and flowers had been laid at the bottom of the tree. There were cards there too. Someone had died there. Ross had heard about the accident. A boy, Thomas Tully, had lost control of his motorbike and had crashed into this tree. Thomas Tully. Ross remembered seeing his photograph in the paper, a smiling boy with a mop of bright red hair. He had still been a teenager, the report said, a boy with a great career in football ahead of him. It has all been snatched away the day his motorbike had crashed into this tree. Ross couldn't take is eyes off that football shirt. It was the very latest top of his favourite team, the best team in the world. It was a really special top, a limited edition. There'd only been a few made. Ross was saving up for that very football shirt himself. And here it was, pinned to a tree.

It was such a waste. That football shirt was made to be worn. Worn by a boy like him. A boy like Ross.

Ross gasped. What was he thinking? He drew his eyes away from the tree, got back on his bike and pedalled home.

The first thing he did when he got home was to take his tin from under his bed and count his money, He's never have enough money for that football shirt. It had taken him ages to save this much. He should just ask his mum and dad for the money, but of course he couldn't do that. Money was tight at the moment. Mum only worked part-time, and Dad wasn't even sure if he'd have a job for much longer. No, he couldn't ask them for the money. He'd just have to keep saving.

But that night, as he lay in his bed, he dreamt of the football shirt. He dreamt of it pinned to that tree, wishing it were anywhere else but there. He woke up and heard the rain battering against his window and he thought about his shirt again. He thought about it as if it was almost human, cold and wet, wishing it was warm and dry. He felt sorry for it. It didn't want to be there stuck to that tree.

The next day on his way to school, he passed the tree again, and there was the shirt, soaking wet, glistening in the early morning sun. It seemed to shine so brightly against the dark trunk of the tree.

It's a waste, a voice whispered to him. *It shouldn't be there. Tully's dead. He doesn't need or want the shirt any longer, does he?*

Ross dragged himself away from the tree. He went to school, but he didn't listen to any of the lessons, he hardly talked to his friends. All he thought about that day was the football shirt. He couldn't get it out of his mind.

Get started

1. Think about a time when you wanted something so badly. Maybe it was a pair of trainers, a game or something else. Write three or four sentences about this.

2. Could it ever be right to steal anything? Write a few sentences explaining your thoughts about this.

3. If you were Ross's friend and knew how much he wanted that football shirt, what advice would you give to him? Write your advice in a speech bubble.

Try these

1. In your own words, summarise what happened to Thomas Tully.

2. Why was this particularly sad?

3. Why do you think the author uses the phrase 'snatched away' to describe what happened to Thomas Tully's career?

4. As Ross looks at the football shirt pinned to the tree, what thoughts are going through his head?

5. Why can't Ross ask his parents for the money to buy a football shirt?

6. The next morning, as he passes the tree where the shirt is pinned, what does the voice in his head suggest to him?

7. Why can't he concentrate on his lessons that day?

8. As the chapter closes, what do you predict that Ross will do?

Now try these

1. Write a few sentences detailing three things that you predict Ross might do next. Underline the one thing that would make the most interesting story.

2. Begin to plan the next chapter in this book. It should include one of your ideas from Question 1. You might want to storyboard each key event in your chapter. Make sure your ideas will hook in the reader. Will it include suspense? Will there be danger? Will Ross have difficult decision to make? Will someone see him?

3. Now write your chapter, always rereading and checking for correct punctuation and effective sentences and vocabulary.

4. Read your chapter to a friend and listen to theirs. Comment on each other's stories; what you liked and what could be written better.

Biography (2)

Read the extract from **'Swimming the Dream'** by **Ellie Simmonds** and then answer the following questions.

Ellie Simmonds is a Paralympic swimmer and winner of five gold medals.

All About Me

I've got achondroplasia, which is sometimes called dwarfism. It doesn't effect me in a big way, but there are lots of little things that have an impact on the way I live. I've got a lot of stools in the kitchen and bathroom because I find it hard to reach things, and if I go to the supermarket on my own I have to ask strangers to get things down from the shelves for me. It's hard if I want to look at something like a magazine because sometimes I just want to flick through it first, but if I've asked someone to get it down for me it's embarrassing to have to ask them to put it back again. It's silly things like that which are hard.

I remember staying at my aunt's house when I was I was younger. It's quite an old place and has the old latch doors. When my cousins shut the doors after them I couldn't get out – well, not easily. I could just about about get my fingertips to knock the latch off to open the doors. It's these sorts of things that you take for granted, which you might not normally think about – like not being able to have shoes that you want and having to have all your clothes altered. My feet are only a size two, and sometimes shop assistants put me into children's shoes – but I don't want flowery babyish shoes, I want teenager-looking shoes in a small size.

I think that, and having to wait for new clothes to be altered, are probably the things that I find most annoying. When I buy new clothes, I want to wear them straight away so it's very frustrating when they don't fit me as they are.

I'm quite lucky though, because everyone at primary school just saw me for who I was and I don't think they took any notice of my disability really, which is exactly what I wanted. When I went to secondary school, I was given some learning support – a teaching assistant who'd help me. I didn't like it because I felt that is separated me from everyone else. I've always just wanted to be with my friends, a regular member of the class, and the extra help made me feel different. The school was good though, because they realised straight away that the support wasn't right for me, so they left me to it. They kept an eye on me and told me to ask for help if I needed it, but otherwise I wasn't given any special treatment. I've always had the just-get-on-with-life approach, and my friends and school have generally been the same. They all just see me as Ellie.

Get started

Discuss these questions and complete the tasks with a partner.

1. Who is your favourite pop star or sportsperson?

2. What do you know about them? Think of five facts for each person.

3. How did you find out information about them?

4. Has there ever been a book written about them? A TV programme? A film?

5. Remind each other of the difference between an autobiography and a biography.

Try these

1. In your own words, summarise Ellie's early days at primary school. What was school like for her?

2. What is most frustrating for Ellie when she buys clothes?

3. Research the condition achondroplasia. Give an example of how simple things might be difficult for people with this condition.

4. Ellie remembers staying at her aunt's house. What was the problem for her?

5. What other problems does she face?

6. Why didn't she like working with a teaching assistant?

Now try these

1. You are going to write a piece of autobiographical writing, describing a typical school day or Saturday. While you should include key moments or events in the day, you should also try to include your thoughts, feelings and reflections about the day, much as Ellie does in her autobiography. The emphasis should be firmly on your personal experience.

   Copy this table to help you gather together some notes for your writing.

Key events in the day	
Feelings – for example, what to do you like or dislike about the day? How do certain parts of it make you feel?	
Thoughts and reflections – for example, do you find the day rewarding? How could the day be improved by you or others?	

2. Now write your piece of autobiographical writing using your notes, remembering to write in full sentences. Check that you have used the correct verb tense (present) and that you are writing in the first person.

Descriptive writing

Read the extract from William Shakespeare's **'The Tempest'** as retold by **John Dougherty and Marcela Calderon,** and then answer the following questions.

> Prospero, a sorcerer, and his daughter, Miranda, have been betrayed by Antonio, Prospero's brother. Antonio set them adrift in a boat. They arrived at a distant island and have lived there for 11 years. One day, Prospero sees a ship sailing by carrying his brother. He decides to use his magic to bring his brother to justice.

Spring turned into summer, and summer into autumn. Autumn became winter, and winter became spring. The years rolled by. And then, one night, a ship came.

Prospero saw the light of its lanterns, shining in the distance, and his magic told him who was aboard. Standing on a high cliff, he stretched his hand out towards the ship, and began to mutter.

The sky grew darker. The waves began to roll and swell. From nowhere came a mighty wind. The clouds burst; cold, hard, heavy rain pounded the ship. Lightning flashed; thunder boomed. The ship was tossed high, like a toy, and swept low, the mountainous sea driving it towards the island.

Prospero smiled grimly. "Ariel!" he said. "That ship carries Alonso, King of Naples. His son and his brother are with him. My treacherous brother Antonio and my noble friend Gonzalo are also aboard. Fly to it and make the passengers think it's sinking. Bring them safely to my island and bring the king's son to me. Go!"

On the desk of the ship, all was chaos.

"Take in the topsail!" yelled the bosun, battling against the wind.

"Bosun!" shouted King Alonso, "where's the ship's master?"

"Get below!" ordered the bosun, as lightning flashed around him. "You're getting in the way!"

"Remember who you are talking to!" Gonzalo shouted, above the roaring of the storm.

"When the storm pays attention to the king, so will I!" the bosun bawled. "Now shut up and get below!"

"Shut up yourself, peasant!" bellowed Sebastian, the king's brother.

"*Get to work or get below*!" the bosun yelled, hauling in the sails.

"Aha!" thought Ariel. "The king and his men are adding to the confusion. Let's see what I can do do to help them!"

Faster than light Ariel flew, from bow to stern; from port to starboard; from deck to mast to wheel. Flames flared and noises boomed and crashed in the spirit's wake, until it seemed to the terrified passengers that the whole world was ablaze. There came a dreadful cracking, splitting sound; and the sailors froze in fear.

"The ship's breaking up!" shouted Ferdinand, the king's son. With that, he leapt into the sea.

"Ferdinand!" shouted King Alonso, plunging in after him.

Whether to help the king, or to flee the ship, the rest of the king's men followed.

Get started

1. Write down some facts you know about William Shakespeare. If you don't know any, research who he was and then write three facts about him.

2. What is a tempest? What happens during one?

3. What is a play? What makes it different from a story or a poem?

4. Name three other plays that Shakespeare wrote.

Try these

1. How does the author tell us that time has passed?

2. How does Prospero know who is on board?

3. What do you think Prospero is muttering?

4. What happens to the weather and the ship?

5. What orders does Prospero give to his servant Ariel?

6. What is happening on the ship?

7. What does Ferdinand do and why?

8. By the end of the extract, where are the sailors and the king's men?

Now try these

1. Reread the extract and draw a comic strip to show what is happening on the island, at sea and on the boat.

2. Look carefully at the illustration of the ship in the tempest. In your own words and in the past tense, describe the scene as if you were watching it from the island. Describe the sea, the sky, the ship and what the men are doing.

Persuasive letter

This letter was written to the local newspaper in response to the news that a new high-speed train link is going to pass through the village and that therefore, the village green will have to go. Many angry villagers wrote to the newspaper with their complaints and this is just one of the letters.

Read the letter carefully and answer the following questions.

Claire Smith
6 The Green
Mellingham

Name and address of the sender – the person who writes the letter

Mellingham Chronicle
12 Station Road
Mellingham

Name and address of the addressee – the person to receive letter

28 November 2017

The date

Dear Sir,

The salutation (greeting) – followed by a comma

I am writing in complaint about the recent news to hit the village. I am a local resident and have lived here for 25 years. It has come to my knowledge that you are considering a proposal to allow the high-speed train route to pass through our village. Surely you cannot be serious?

The introduction

There are many reasons why this should not happen.

Firstly, the village green is the centre of our community: the place where children play, where the school and church fete is held and where we gather for the annual summer barbeque.

The main body

Secondly, the green is an historic site, having been recorded in early-medieval church records as a place where farmers might graze their sheep.

Lastly, it is a beauty spot and a safe and secure place for the elderly to walk and enjoy feeding the ducks and chatting to one another.

The conclusion

I hope you will reconsider your plans in the light of this letter.
I look forward to hearing from you as soon as possible.

The closing

Yours faithfully,
Claire Smith

Signature – don't forget to sign your letter!

Get started

1. Why do you think that people write to newspapers about their concerns?

2. What is Claire hoping to gain from writing the letter?

3. Have you ever felt so strongly about a subject that you wanted to take action? Do you know anyone who has? Have you or one of your ever wanted to complain about something to your teacher or head teacher? Write a few sentences explaining what happened.

4. Look at the way in which the letter is set out and remind yourself of the structure.

Try these

1. What are the town council considering?

2. Who is complaining about this?

3. List the arguments that Claire makes against the proposal.

4. In your opinion, which is the most important argument she makes?

5. Which do you think is not really important?

Now try these

1. List three reasons why the high-speed train link should go ahead.

2. Using the same letter layout, write the short reply that Claire received back from the town council. Use the arguments or reasons you came up with in answer to Question 1.

3. Write a short letter of complaint to your head teacher about something that concerns you in school.

Discursive writing

Read the article **'Nessie or Not?'** written by **Chris Whitney** and answer the following questions.

Title may be a question	**Nessie or Not?**

For many years, people have debated the existence, or not, of the Loch Ness Monster. The debate **continues** to this day. Views vary and strong arguments for and against abound.

Opening statement sums up argument to be discussed

Written mostly in simple present tense

For example, **some people** strongly believe that they have personally sighted the monster swimming in the 'loch'. These sightings have occurred over time and have been widely reported. George Miller, a local resident, remembers watching 'Nessie' in the lake as a small boy. Other people, **experts** in their field, have photographic and sonic evidence which claims to back up their views and beliefs.

Argument is seen from both sides

Written in the third person

Viewpoints presented with reasons and evidence, and developed in paragraphs

Generic statements are often followed by specific examples

However, these views are not shared by everyone and opinions differ as to the existence of a 'monster' in the loch. There are claims, for example, that both photographic and sonic evidence is fake – it has been fabricated. It is the work of those who would have us believe in 'Nessie'.

Relationships between paragraphs and sections give structure to whole text

Generic participants (for example, experts, biologists)

Varied sentence openers

Individual paragraphs vary in length but have a clear focus

Links made between opening and conclusion

Text ends with a summary and a statement of recommendation or conclusion

Furthermore, expert **biologists** claim that conditions in the loch would not be able to sustain life. They have sent divers to search the depths of the loch – divers who have returned empty handed, reporting no trace of the monster at all. Some people have gone so far as to say that the 'sightings' themselves are the product of an over-excitable imagination.

Complex sentences with varied use of adverbials to connect ideas

Therefore, it is possible to see that there is a wide range of opinions for and against the existence of the Loch Ness Monster. The views presented in this article leave you with a choice – do you believe in Nessie?

Get started

1. Have you ever heard of the Loch Ness monster before? Have you heard rumours and stories of other creatures that are supposed to roam the countryside here or abroad, or that inhabit rivers and lakes?

2. Do you believe that such monsters could exist?

3. What about life on other planets? Do you believe in aliens?

4. Discuss this with the person sitting next to you. What do they believe?

Try these

1. What do you notice about the way the argument for or against Nessie is set out?

2. How many points are made for and against on each side of the discussion?

3. Which do you think is the best argument supporting the view that Nessie exists?

4. Which do you think is the best argument opposing the view that Nessie exists?

5. How is the discussion concluded?

6. In what tense should discursive writing be written?

Now try these

1. Imagine that there have been surveys to find out people's opinion on the following topics:

   • Sport should not be compulsory in schools.

   • Animals should not perform in circuses.

2. Choose one of the topics to write a discussion text about. Use the table to help you write your notes.

Supporting the view (For)	Opposing the view (Against)

3. Give your discussion text a title and write the opening statement. Remember that the opening statement sums up the argument to be discussed.

4. Continue with your argument, making the supporting (for) and opposing (against) points.

5. Write the conclusion. State what you agree with, what you disagree with and a possible recommendation or line of action.

Discursive writing

A. Write a piece of discursive writing on the following proposal: 'School should start and finish earlier in the day'. Use the planner to help you.

Title or proposal: _____	
Introduction / opening statement	
Supporting arguments	1._____ 2. _____ 3. _____
Opposing arguments	1._____ 2. _____ 3. _____
Conclusion with short summary and recommend- ation	

Descriptive writing

B. Choose one of the following titles and write a descriptive paragraph. Use the planner to help you.

- A deserted street at night

- A busy street during the day

What I can see	Words or phrases to describe

Persuasive letter

C. Write a persuasive letter to one of the following:

- a supermarket – after the food you bought there made you ill
- to the local council – after rubbish bins were not emptied last week.

Use the checklist to help you.

> **Letter conventions checklist:**
>
> - Address in top right-hand corner
>
> - Date under this
>
> - Greeting – do you know the person's name?
>
> - Use paragraphs to structure what you want to say
>
> - Signing off – check you have used the right form